JUV/
GV
721.5
.B87
2002
SCOTTS
Chicago Public Library
W9-AFT-912
R0401262405
Great moments in the Olympics
JUN 2004
CHICAGO PUBLIC LIBRARY
SCOTTSDALE BRANCH
4101 W. 79TH ST 60652

Great Moments in **SPORTS**

GREAT MOMENTS IN THE OLYMPICS

by Michael Burgan

WORLD ALMANAC® LIBRARY

Please visit our web site at: www.worldalmanaclibrary.com
For a free color catalog describing World Almanac® Library's list of high-quality books and multimedia programs, call 1-800-848-2928 (USA) or 1-800-387-3178 (Canada).
World Almanac® Library's fax: (414) 332-3567.

Library of Congress Cataloging-in-Publication Data

Burgan, Michael.
Great moments in the Olympics / by Michael Burgan— North American ed.
p. cm. — (Great moments in sports)
Summary: Recounts ten high points in the history of the Olympics, including Jesse Owens winning four gold medals against the Nazis, Nadia Comaneci receiving perfect scores in gymnastics in 1976, and Eric Heiden's performance at the 1980 Winter games.
Includes bibliographical references and index.
ISBN 0-8368-5348-2 (lib. bdg.)
ISBN 0-8368-5362-8 (softcover)
1. Olympics—History—Juvenile literature. 2. Athletes—Biography—Juvenile literature.
[1. Olympics—History.] I. Title. II. Great moments in sports (Milwaukee, Wis.)
GV721.53.B87 2002
796.48—dc21 2002016870

This North American edition first published in 2002 by
World Almanac® Library
330 West Olive Street, Suite 100
Milwaukee, WI 53212 USA

An Editorial Directions book
Editor: Lucia Raatma
Photo researcher: Image Select International Ltd.
Copy editor: Melissa McDaniel
Proofreader: Sarah De Capua
Indexer: Tim Griffin
Art direction, design, and page production: The Design Lab
World Almanac® Library editorial direction: Mark J. Sachner
World Almanac® Library art direction: Tammy Gruenewald
World Almanac® Library production: Susan Ashley and Jessica L. Yanke

Photographs ©: Getty Images, cover, 3, 4, 5; Corbis, 6, 7; Getty Images, 8, 9, 10, 11, 12, 13, 14; Corbis, 15; Getty Images, 16; Corbis, 17, 18, 19, 20, 21; Getty Images, 22, 23; Corbis, 25, 26; Getty Images, 27; Corbis, 28, 29, 30, 31, 32, 33; Getty Images, 34, 35, 36; Corbis, 37; Getty Images, 38, 39, 40, 41; Reuters/Popperfoto, 42; AFP, 43; Reuters/Popperfoto, 44; Getty Images, 45; Corbis, 46 top right, 46 bottom left; Getty Images, 46 bottom right.

Printed in the United States of America

1 2 3 4 5 6 7 8 9 06 05 04 03 02

Opposite: *U.S. speedster Carl Lewis at the 1984 Los Angeles Games, where he took a total of four gold medals. His mastery of the long jump would continue for the next four Summer Olympics and span twelve years. Here, flanked by silver medalist James Beckford of Jamaica and bronze medalist Joe Greene of the United States, Lewis celebrates his final long-jump gold at the 1996 Atlanta games.*

Contents

Introduction

Three athletes stand on raised platforms, their eyes turned upward. In the center, a little higher than the other two, the winner listens intently as the national anthem plays. Around the victor's neck dangles perhaps the most valued prize in all of sports—an Olympic gold medal.

To win that medal, athletes train endless hours, then compete to represent their country. Once on the national team, they find the competition is even fiercer, as only the world's best athletes make it to the Olympics.

The 2002 Winter Olympics in Salt Lake City were marked by a number of controversial decisions. The most highly publicized of these resulted in an Olympic first—the awarding of two sets of gold medals in a single event, pairs figure skating.

The modern Olympic Games began in 1896, when Baron Pierre de Coubertin of France proposed bringing athletes together in a spirit of international harmony and sportsmanship. The baron modeled the Games after the original Olympics, first held in Greece in 776 B.C. The first Games included footraces, chariot races, and boxing. The first modern Games featured track and field, weightlifting, gymnastics, and cycling, and about two hundred athletes from fourteen countries took part.

Every four years since (except during World Wars I and II), athletes have competed for Olympic medals—gold, silver, and bronze. Since 1896, the number of Olympic events has grown to more than three hundred. Women were first allowed to compete in 1912, in swimming. In 1924, the International Olympic Committee introduced separate Winter Games. These were held the same year as the Summer Olympics until 1992. The next Winter Games took place in 1994 and have been held every four years since.

Despite their original intent—to promote goodwill among all the countries of the world—the Olympics have had plenty of controversy. At first only amateur athletes were allowed to compete, and some were disqualified when officials discovered they had received money to play a sport—any sport. U.S. track-and-field champion Jim Thorpe lost his medals from the 1912 Games because he had once played semiprofessional baseball (though the medals were restored years after his death). Starting in the 1980s, pros were allowed to compete, ending the questions over amateur status.

Between the years 1945 and 1991, many political clashes affected the Olympic Games. This was the era of the Cold War, a struggle between the United States and the Soviet Union to influence other countries and promote their own political systems. In 1980, the United States refused to compete in Moscow, the Soviet capital, to protest the 1979 Soviet invasion of Afghanistan. Four years later, the Soviets boycotted the Los Angeles Games, in response to the U.S. boycott.

Countries and athletes have sometimes used the Olympics as a platform to express their concerns to the world. In 1968, African-American athletes Tommie Smith and John Carlos wore black gloves to the podium when they received their medals. They then raised their fists as "The Star-Spangled Banner" played, to protest the treatment of blacks in the United States. At the 2000 Games in Sydney, Australia, sprinter Cathy Freeman, an Aborigine (indigenous Australian), brought attention to the history of strained racial relations in her homeland.

The 1984 L.A. Summer Games (above) were boycotted by the Soviet Union and other Eastern European nations in response to the boycott of the 1980 Moscow games by sixty-two other nations, including the United States.

The most disturbing political conflict at the Olympics came at the 1972 Games in Munich, West Germany. Then, as now, Palestinians were struggling to create a homeland in territory controlled by Israel. During the Games, Palestinian terrorists stormed the dorm where Israeli athletes were staying. Two Israelis were killed and nine others were taken hostage. The Games continued as a shocked world watched the horror unfold on television. When West German officials tried to

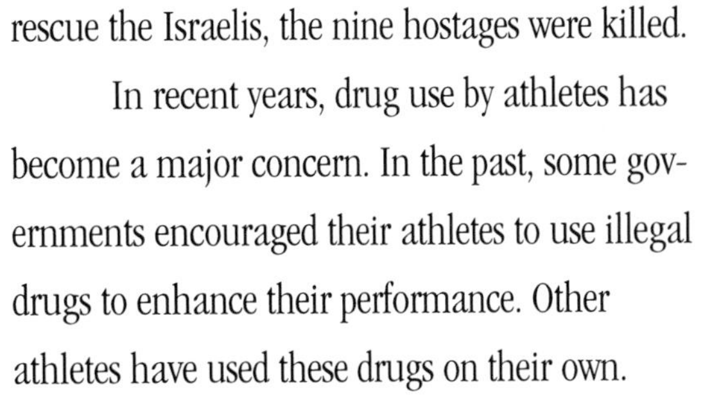

rescue the Israelis, the nine hostages were killed.

In recent years, drug use by athletes has become a major concern. In the past, some governments encouraged their athletes to use illegal drugs to enhance their performance. Other athletes have used these drugs on their own.

Off the playing field, some local Olympic organizers have broken the law by bribing Olympic officials. Like other sports, the Olympics have become a business, and large sums of money are at stake for the city chosen to host the Games.

Even though violence, drugs, and controversy have sometimes marred the Games, the Olympic goal remains the same: to promote harmony and good sportsmanship and reward athletic excellence. Since 1896, the Olympics have produced some of the most memorable accomplishments in sports history. Sometimes those moments have occurred in a flash. Others reflect outstanding performance in several events. Choosing only ten for this book was difficult. Some achievements are so great, no one would argue whether they should be included here. Other great moments are not so clear-cut. The best Olympic feats from both the Summer and Winter Games, from individuals and teams, could fill several books like this one. What follows is one look at ten great Olympic moments.

THE FLYING FINN TAKES FIVE

Paavo Nurmi Wins Five Gold Medals at the 1924 Summer Olympics

At the 1912 Summer Games in Stockholm, Sweden, long-distance runner Hannes Kolehmainen won three gold medals. His victories brought great pride to his homeland of Finland. They also inspired fifteen-year-old Paavo Nurmi, a Finnish farm boy who enjoyed running through the forests near his home, to dedicate his life to running. He would become the greatest long-distance runner the world had seen.

Finnish runner Paavo Nurmi taking the last wall in the 10,000-meter cross-country race at the 1924 Summer Games in Paris.

Nurmi was blessed with an unusually low heartbeat, which gave him tremendous stamina. He also trained hard, doing exercises and running more often than most distance runners of the day. After winning his first race in 1914, he set his sights on running in the 1916 Olympics. World War I, however, forced the cancellation of the Games, so Nurmi's first chance to run for gold didn't come until 1920.

At the 1920 Olympics, held in Antwerp, Belgium, Nurmi did not win a medal in his first event, the 5,000-meter race. But in the 10,000-meter race, Nurmi came back to win after briefly losing the lead, then added two more gold medals in the cross-country events. The legend of the "Flying Finn" had begun.

Nurmi winning the 5,000-meter event at the 1924 Olympics, with Ville Ritola placing second.

World Records and More Medals

After the 1920 Games, Nurmi set his first world record, in the 10,000-meter event. By the end of 1923, he held the records in the mile and 5,000-meter distances as well. He became the only runner ever to hold world records in those three distances at the same time. During his career, he set more than thirty world records. When he ran, Nurmi tried to block out the competition and focus only on the clock. "When you race against time," he said, "you don't have to sprint."

Nurmi knew that the key to winning in long-distance races was to hold the pace steady all the way to the finish line. To do this, he held a stopwatch in his left hand to time his pace.

Entering the 1924 Games in Paris, France, Nurmi was a clear favorite to dominate the long-distance races. He lost the 10,000-meter event to teammate Ville Ritola, but he won the 10,000-meter cross-country race. He also won gold medals as a member of the 3,000-meter and 10,000-meter cross-country team. Nurmi's greatest performance, however, came on July 10, when he was scheduled to run both the 1,500- and the 5,000-meter competitions.

The day was brutally hot, but Nurmi seemed cool. A writer commented that Nurmi looked "as though ice water were being pumped through his veins." He ran the 1,500-meter race in 3:53.6, setting a new Olympic record. Less than two hours later, he ran the 5,000-meter race.

Nurmi's main rival for the event was Ritola. The two Finns raced side by side for about 3,000 meters. Nurmi often checked his stopwatch, wanting to run a pace that would

Paavo Nurmi (center) battling Ville Ritola (left) and Edvin Wide (right) in the 10,000-meter race at the 1928 Olympics.

NINE TIMES A CHAMPION

Paavo Nurmi's winning times for his nine Olympic gold medals

1920	10,000 meters – 31:45.8
	cross-country – 27:15.10
	team cross-country – same time used from individual race
1924	1,500 meters – 3:53.6
	5,000 meters – 14:31.2
	cross-country – 32:54.8
	team cross-country – same time used from individual race
	team 3,000 meters – 8:32.0
1928	10,000 meters – 30:18.8

bring him in just under the Olympic record. Then Ritola burst ahead, forcing Nurmi to sprint after him. Nurmi regained the lead, but Ritola inched past with less than 500 meters to go. With one last kick, Nurmi took the lead again. He won by a stride, and his time of 14:31.2 set a new Olympic record.

His performance in the heat that day, and his five gold medals for the Games, made Nurmi an international sports hero. The next year, he toured the United States and won fifty-three of fifty-five races. When asked about his success,

Nurmi said that his well-conditioned body was just "a piece of rubber." It was concentration and the will to win that mattered. "All that I am," he said, "I am because of my mind."

Last Medals

Nurmi appeared in one more Olympics, running in Amsterdam, the Netherlands, in 1928. He had thought about skipping the Games, but he knew more medals would boost his popularity in the United States, where he often ran. He finished second in the 5,000- and 3,000-meter races, then won another gold in the 10,000-meter event.

Nurmi wanted to race again in 1932, looking for gold in the marathon. Just before the Games began, however, he was accused of accepting money for a race in Germany. Nurmi denied the charge and tried to clear his name, but he could not regain his amateur status.

Although his Olympic career was over, Nurmi had set the record for career gold medals—nine. He now shares this record with U.S. swimmer Mark Spitz, U.S. track star Carl Lewis, and Russian gymnast Larissa Latynina. Nurmi received many honors during his life and after his death in 1973. He has appeared on Finnish postage stamps and bank notes and was the subject of an opera. Perhaps no athlete has ever been more cherished by his homeland than the Flying Finn.

ADVICE TO YOUNG ATHLETES

On his 1925 trip to the United States, Paavo Nurmi spoke on the radio and explained his ideas about athletic competition:

My greetings to the youths of this country are, that they practice athletics on principle, without expecting immediate rewards. One must learn to win modestly, and to lose with good spirit. This indeed is the mark of a true athlete. Above all, one must never be concerned about rewards. In a race always follow your own plan, and be not concerned about your rivals, whether they are ahead of you or behind you.

At the 1952 Summer Olympics in Helsinki, Nurmi was given the honor of lighting the Olympic flame.

JESSE AND THE NAZIS

Jesse Owens Wins Four Gold Medals at the 1936 Berlin Olympics

The world was on the brink of its second global conflict, and to German dictator Adolf Hitler, the 1936 Summer Olympics were his Games. He wanted to show the world how his Nazi Party had made Germany a great nation. He also planned to showcase the Nazis' ideology of Aryan supremacy and demonstrate to the world that Germans were the finest athletes, the strongest and smartest people, in the world. Hitler was convinced that Jews, blacks, and members of other "non-Aryan" ethnic groups and races were inferior.

Jesse Owens soaring in the long jump event at the 1936 Olympics in Berlin.

Before the Games, some nations—including the United States—debated whether they should send a team to Berlin. They did not want to appear to support Hitler and his racist theories and policies. Still, when the Games began, more than 4,000 athletes from forty-nine nations, including the United States, were in Germany.

One man representing the United States was Jesse Owens. As an African American, he was one of the "inferior" people Hitler so detested. In track and field, however, Owens was already a legend. At the 1935 Big Ten track-and-field championships, he had set three world records and tied another—within one hour! Known as "the world's fastest human," Owens was favored to do well at the Olympics, whether the Nazis liked it or not.

Two Events, Two Gold Medals

Owens's first event in Berlin was the 100-meter dash. He easily won his qualifying races, and his five opponents in the finals included a German. When the starting gun sounded, the runners began as a pack, but about 30 meters out, Owens took the lead. Owens sprinted down the track in 10.3 seconds, tying the Olympic record. As Owens received his gold medal, Hitler was reported to have said, "The Americans should be ashamed of themselves, letting Negroes win their medals for them."

Next up for Owens was the long jump. During the qualifying round, he fouled on his first two tries. Before his last attempt, he received some advice from an unlikely source: German long jumper Luz Long. Despite the official Nazi attitude toward blacks, Long came over to help Owens, telling him to jump before he hit the takeoff board. Years later Owens described the scene: "[Long] even laid his towel down at exactly the place from which I was to jump. It was so simple!" Owens took the suggestions and hit a legal jump.

In the finals, Long and Owens dueled for the gold. Each set new Olympic records, closing in on 26 feet (7.9 meters). Then, on his last jump, Owens soared 26 feet 5½ inches (8.01 m), winning his second gold medal.

Above: *Owens won the gold medal for the 100-meter race as well as the 200-meter, the long jump, and the 4 x 100-meter relay.*

WAS JESSE SNUBBED?

For years, people believed that Adolf Hitler snubbed Jesse Owens after he won the 100-meter race. The day before, Hitler had invited several German medal winners to his box—but not two African-American winners. Olympic officials then asked the German leader to invite either all medal winners to his box, or none. Hitler chose the latter, perhaps because he did not want to shake hands with non-Aryan athletes, but the snub was not apparently directed specifically at Owens. Still, Hitler often left the stadium when Owens was competing. Asked about the incident years later, Owens said of Hitler, "I didn't come there to shake hands with him."

Long rushed over to congratulate his new American friend.

Two More Records

In the 200 meters, Owens won his first heat in 21.1 seconds, setting a new Olympic record. His teammate Mack Robinson (older brother of baseball great Jackie Robinson) tied the mark in a later race. The two record holders met in the finals, but that race belonged to Owens. He ran the 200 in 20.7 seconds, giving him another Olympic record and his third gold medal.

TASTING GLORY

In his autobiography *Jesse*, Jesse Owens describes winning the gold medal in the long jump.

I hit the takeoff board. Leaped up, up, up— . . . I reached to the sky as I leaped for the farthest part of the ground.

The farthest—

I was on the earth once again. I felt the dirt and the sand of the pit in my shoes and on my legs. Instinctively, I fell forward, my elbows digging in, the tremendous velocity of my jump forcing sand into my mouth.

It tasted good. Because, almost instinctively, I sensed it was sand from a part of the pit which no one had ever reached before.

Owens, in lane four (second from right), having just passed the baton to Ralph Metcalfe in the 4 x 100-meter relay, which the U.S. team went on to win.

Owens's last event was the 4 x 100-meter relay. He ran the first leg and handed off the baton with a sizable lead. Each U.S. runner after him widened that advantage, and the four Americans finished with a combined time of 39.8 seconds. Owens had helped the team set a new world record, and he left the arena that day with his fourth gold medal.

No matter how Hitler and other Nazi leaders felt, the Germans embraced Owens and his incredible performance. All together, African-American athletes won almost one-quarter of all the U.S. medals in the Games. Their performances brought honor to themselves, their team, and their nation—and were a slap in the face of Hitler's racist politics.

Unfortunately, Owens still had to confront racism back home in the United States. He was forced to ride freight elevators in plush hotels, and to make money, he agreed to race dogs and horses. "You can't eat four gold medals," he once said. Over time, however, he won greater respect and recognition. In 1990, ten years after his death, Owens was awarded the Congressional Medal of Honor, a tribute to his sports accomplishments and his dedication to civil rights.

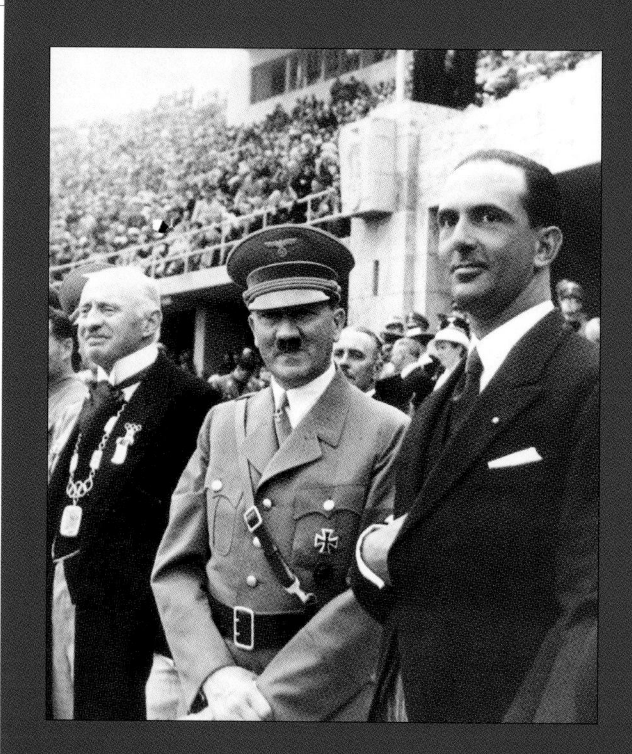

Above: *Nazi Germany's dictator Adolf Hitler, shown here with Prince Umberto of Italy (right), had the misconception that his nation's athletes would dominate the 1936 Olympic Games. Jesse Owens helped discredit the notion of Aryan racial superiority.*

MORE PREJUDICE IN BERLIN

Although the Nazis considered people of many ethnic backgrounds inferior to Germans, they directed most of their hatred toward Jews. Unfortunately, at the 1936 Games, some U.S. Olympic officials seemed to support Nazi Germany and its anti-Semitic policies. Marty Glickman and Sam Stoller, two Jewish-American sprinters, made the U.S. Olympic team and traveled to Berlin. But when it came time for their event, the 400-meter relay, the two runners were replaced by Jesse Owens and Ralph Metcalfe. The U.S. track coach had argued that Owens and Metcalfe were faster runners, but Glickman and many others believed he and Stoller were bumped because they were Jews. Years later, Glickman gratefully recalled what Owens had told a U.S. coach: "Let Marty and Sam run, they deserve it. I've won my medals." Owens, however, had no choice. He ran the race, and Glickman and Stoller went home without competing.

THE LONGEST JUMP

Bob Beamon Smashes the World Record for the Long Jump at the 1968 Games

For twenty-five years, the great track-and-field star Jesse Owens held the world record in the long jump: 26 feet, $8\frac{1}{4}$ inches (8.15 m). The record finally fell in 1960, when Ralph Boston beat Owens's mark by about three inches.

For the next eight years, Boston and Soviet jumper Igor Ter-Ovanesyan took turns nudging the record up several more inches, with Boston finally reaching 27 feet $4\frac{3}{4}$ inches (8.36 m) in 1965. That record still stood when Bob Beamon made his first jump at the 1968 Summer Olympics in Mexico City.

Bob Beamon made Olympic history with a record-breaking long jump at the 1968 Summer Games in Mexico City.

That year, Beamon had emerged as one of the world's top long jumpers, winning all but one of his events. Jumping indoors, he won the national college championship. Outdoors, he took the Amateur Athletic Union championship, then finished first at the U.S. Olympic trials, beating Boston, a two-time Olympic medal winner. In his mind, Beamon thought he could set a new world record at the Olympics.

Early Troubles

At Mexico City, Beamon faced stiff competition from Boston, Ter-Ovanesyan, and the defending gold-medal winner, Lynn

Long jumper Ralph Boston (above) held the world record as Bob Beamon headed to the 1968 Olympics.

Davies of Great Britain. Beamon also struggled during the qualifying round. Twice he fouled, his toes landing past the takeoff board as he began his jump. As German long jumper Luz Long had advised American Jesse Owens at the 1936 Olympics, Boston suggested that Beamon take off a few inches before the board on the last jump, which would ensure he recorded a clean leap. Beamon took the advice and made the medal round with a jump of 26 feet 10½ inches (8.2 m).

Still, Beamon was under pressure—some of it his own doing. He had told reporters he could break 28 feet (8.54 m), even though no one had yet come close to that mark. His troubles in the qualifying round also worried him. Beamon and the other jumpers, however, did have one advantage. At an altitude of more than 7,000 feet (2,135 m), Mexico City has thin air—air with less oxygen. Although the thin air was a problem for distance runners, making it harder for them to breathe, the air seemed to offer less wind resistance and thus boost the performance of athletes competing in short track races and the jumping events.

Lynn Davies, here making a gold-medal jump in the 1964 Games in Tokyo, was tough competition for Bob Beamon.

A Dream of a Leap

October 18, the day of the long-jump finals, was cool. A 2-mile-per-hour (3.2-kilometer-per-hour) breeze blew at the jumpers' backs. Under track-and-field rules, if the wind had been stronger, a record-setting jump that day would not have counted.

Beamon watched as the first three competitors fouled on their first jump. Then it was his turn. At 6 feet 3 inches (191 centimeters) he had long, powerful legs that pushed him down the track with amazing speed. He hit the takeoff board and leapt. In the air, his arms and legs moved as if he were walking hurriedly across a busy street. Halfway across the sand pit, he pulled his legs up close to his chest to finish the jump. Landing on his rear, he quickly bounded up. "I was very upset I had landed on my bottom instead

FROM JESSE TO BOB

World long-jump records from 1935 until 1968

Distance	Athlete	Date
29 feet 2½ inches	Bob Beamon	Oct. 18, 1968
27 feet 4¾ inches	Igor Ter-Ovanesyan	Oct. 19, 1967
27 feet 4¾ inches	Ralph Boston	May 29, 1965
27 feet 4¼ inches	Ralph Boston	Sept. 12, 1964
27 feet 3¼ inches	Ralph Boston	Aug. 15, 1964
27 feet 3¼ inches	Igor Ter-Ovanesyan	June 10, 1962
27 feet 2 inches	Ralph Boston	July 16, 1961
27 feet ½ inch	Ralph Boston	May 27, 1961
26 feet 11 inches	Ralph Boston	Aug. 12, 1960
26 feet 8¼ inches	Jesse Owens	May 25, 1935

of landing on my legs," Beamon later said.

Even with that ungraceful landing, everyone in the stadium knew Beamon had hit a good jump. After leaving the pit, he bounced up and down and gleefully waved his arms. It took several minutes, however, for Beamon and the audience to learn just how special his performance had been. The electronic measuring system used for the long jump was too short to measure the leap. Officials had to find an old-fashioned steel measuring tape. Finally Beamon's distance flashed on the scoreboard: 8.90 meters, or 29 feet 2½ inches. Beamon collapsed in joy, realizing what he had done. "Tell me I'm not dreaming," he said in his relief and joy.

Beamon had beaten the old world record by almost 2 feet (.61 m). With one leap, he became the first athlete to soar past 28 and then 29 feet. Beamon's new record was immediately called one of the greatest achievements ever in track and field.

Beamon never again came close to jumping 29 feet. The record that some said could never be broken finally was, by Mike Powell, who jumped 29 feet 4½ inches (8.95 m) in 1991. Beamon's jump, however, is still an Olympic record, and it helped him win a place in the Olympic Hall of Fame.

Above: *On the victory stand, Bob Beamon proudly wore the gold medal while fellow American jumper Ralph Boston (left) took bronze and Klaus Beer (right) of East Germany took silver.*

ANOTHER CHANCE

As a kid, Bob Beamon roamed the streets of Queens, New York, frequently getting into trouble. At age fourteen, he joined a gang and was arrested. "I remember fear clutching at my stomach as I stood before the judge," he later said. Beamon, however, was lucky. "My grandmother stepped up for me and said she would take responsibility for me and a compassionate juvenile judge took a chance and gave me one. They were getting ready to send me away to do real time, but they sent me instead to a juvenile alternative day school. And I guess that was the beginning of my turnaround." Beamon turned to track and field in high school, eventually setting a state record in the long jump and then moving on to Olympic greatness.

Since ending his competitive career, Beamon has dedicated himself to trying to help other young people avoid the mistakes he made and giving youthful offenders a second chance.

A "STOLEN" GOLD

At the 1972 Olympics, the U.S. Basketball Team Loses for the First Time Ever

Basketball became an Olympic sport in 1936, and from the beginning, the U.S. team dominated. Using top college and Amateur Athletic Union (AAU) players, the U.S. squad won the first gold medal by defeating Canada, 19–8. The games were played outdoors, and Olympic officials had tried to ban players over 6 feet 2 inches (188 cm) until the Americans complained.

A brief moment of joy for the U.S. basketball team before the game clock was reset and the Soviet Union went on to claim the win.

Over the years, the U.S. teams included such future Hall of Famers as Bill Russell, Jerry West, and Oscar Robertson. The Americans took a fifty-three-game winning streak into the 1972 Munich Games, but coach Hank Iba was not guaranteeing an eighth consecutive gold medal. His team did not have the country's best college player, University of California at Los Angeles (UCLA) center Bill Walton, who had chosen to sit out the Games. And Iba knew that the competition was getting better. "Look at the Russian team," Iba told reporters. "It's a national team. The players have been playing together for more than 700 games since the last Olympics."

It wasn't a coincidence that Iba mentioned the team from the Soviet Union. It had won two silvers and a bronze at the previous three Olympics, and the Soviet players were among the best in Europe. The Cold War also magnified the importance of the strong Soviet team. There was great world tension between the Soviet Union and the United States at that time. That tension led to much rivalry and competition.

Another Gold-Medal Game

As the Olympic basketball tournament began, Iba's team easily won its first three games. Brazil, however, gave the Americans a challenge, keeping the game close and losing by only 7 points. After that, led by guard Tom Henderson and center Dwight Jones, the United States team rolled over its opponents. On September 10, the Americans prepared for the gold-medal game. Waiting on the other side of the court were the Russians.

The Soviet team took a 7–0 lead and led by five at halftime. During the second half, with the score still close, the play turned rough. Jones, the best U.S. player in the tournament, wrestled with Ivan Dvorni for a loose ball. Both players were ejected. A few seconds later, a Soviet player knocked Jim Brewer to the floor. Brewer never returned to the game.

With less than a minute to play, the Americans trailed 49–46. Jim Forbes hit a jump shot for the Americans, closing the gap to one. With six seconds left, Doug Collins intercepted a pass and raced for a layup. Before he could score, a Soviet player fouled him hard, leaving Collins dazed as he went to the free throw line. Just three seconds remained. Collins made his first shot, tying the score. As he made the second shot, the scorer's buzzer went off in error, signaling the end of the game. That was the beginning of the strangest ending ever in an international basketball game.

A stunned and dejected U.S. basketball team after losing the gold to the Soviet squad.

Three Tries to Win

With the score 50–49, the Soviets tried to call a time-out. International rules did not allow a time-out after made free throws. One official instructed the Russians to inbound the ball. They did, then headed for the scorer's table to protest the denial of the time-out. The Russians claimed they had called for the time-out before

USELESS PROTESTS

A five-man committee heard the U.S. protest of the Soviet victory and voted 3–2 to deny it. The members voting against the United States came from Poland, Cuba, and Hungary—all countries that were heavily controlled or influenced by the Soviet government. The two members voting for the United States came from Italy and Puerto Rico. The Americans also complained that R. William Jones, the FIBA official who had stepped into the controversy, had no authority at the Olympics. The U.S. position was technically correct, but Jones was a powerful man in international basketball. No one connected with the game wanted to overrule him. Once again, the U.S. claim was rejected.

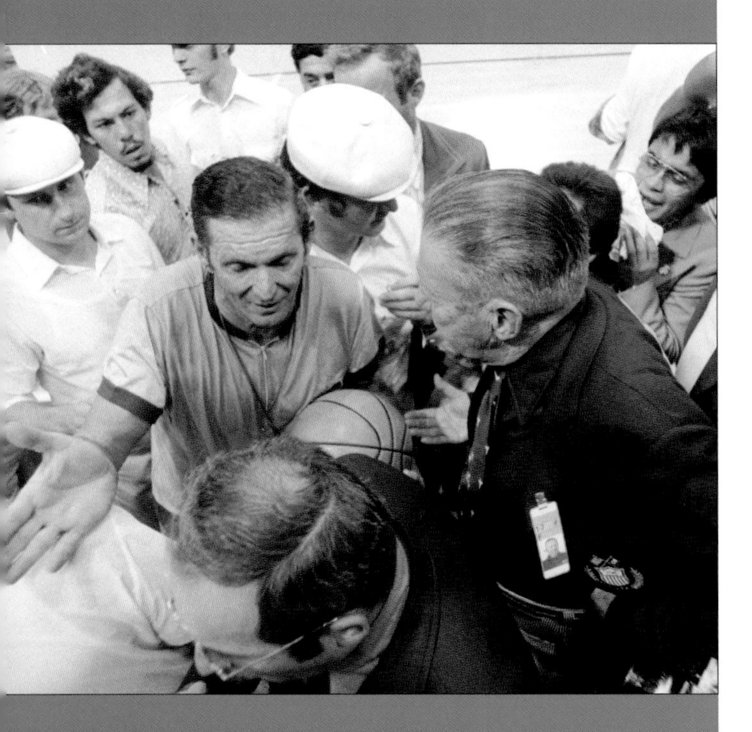

the foul shots. As the discussion went on, the clock seemed to run out, giving the Americans the win. Another official, however, had stopped the clock with one second left. He had been confused by the earlier buzzer and the activity at the scorer's table. Now the officials reset the clock to three seconds and let the Soviets inbound the ball again.

Tom McMillen, a 6-foot-11-inch (210-cm) forward, waved his arms to block the pass. The ball never reached its target, the clock ran out, and once again the Americans thought they had won. This time, an official from the International Amateur Basketball Federation (FIBA) stepped in. He ruled that the clock had not been reset properly before the second inbound play. Once again, the officials put three seconds on the clock. Once again, the Soviets had the ball.

McMillen again tried to block the inbound pass, but this time the Soviet player made a clean pass down court. Two Americans were defending Aleksander Belov, and all three went for the ball. Belov caught it and scored just before the buzzer sounded. The Soviets had won, 51–50.

Everyone in the arena and watching the game on television was stunned and confused—except for the celebrating Soviets. Coach Iba said, "I've never seen anything like

Above: *U.S. coach Hank Iba argued furiously with game referees, but his objections were overruled.*

this in all my years of basketball." The Americans filed a protest, but the final score stood. The Americans had finally lost an Olympic basketball game. Later, a review of a tape of the game's last few seconds showed that the referees had missed two calls against the Soviets—a three-second lane violation and an inbound violation. Either call would have given the Americans the ball—and the game.

Years later, Doug Collins reflected on his experience in 1972. "Nothing comes close to the feeling of a twenty-one-year-old kid playing for his country and winning the gold," he said. "Nothing comes close to the feeling I should've had if they hadn't taken it away from me."

Above: *When officials ruled that the victory belonged to the Soviets, the team was quick to celebrate.*

SILVER NUMBERS

Results for the U.S. basketball team at the 1972 Olympics

USA	66	Czechoslovakia	35
USA	81	Australia	55
USA	67	Cuba	48
USA	61	Brazil	54
USA	96	Egypt	31
USA	72	Spain	56
USA	99	Japan	33
USA	68	Italy	38
Soviet Union	51	USA	50

LUCKY SEVEN

Mark Spitz Wins Seven Gold Medals at the 1972 Summer Olympics

Mark Spitz spent his early years training to be a swimming champion. After learning to swim at six years old, he began competing at eight. From that young age, Spitz spent hours in the pool, practicing both sprints and long distance. He mastered all the strokes but excelled at the butterfly, the most difficult competitive stroke.

By the time he was eighteen, Spitz had broken twenty-eight U.S. records and ten world records. Going into the 1968 Summer Games in Mexico City, Spitz brashly asserted he would win six gold medals—one in every event he was swimming.

Eighteen-year-old Mark Spitz at the 1968 Olympics in Mexico City, where he won two gold medals.

That self-confidence—or arrogance—turned off some of his teammates and reporters, and Spitz did not live up to his prediction. Still, he did take home four medals, including two golds. After the Games, Spitz entered Indiana University, where he continued to perfect his skills.

"Mark the Shark"

Before the 1972 Games in Munich, Germany, Spitz didn't make any predictions about his performance, but everyone expected him to win several gold medals. His first event was the 200-meter butterfly. At the 1968 Games, Spitz had finished last in this race, but now he was considered the favorite. Spitz's time was 2:00.7, which gave him the gold and a new world record.

The same day, he won his second gold medal as a member of the 4 x 400-meter freestyle relay team. As the anchor, he helped the team set a new world record of 3:26.42.

The next day, Spitz returned to the water for the 200-meter freestyle. Going into the last lap, he trailed teammate Steve Genter, but an extra burst of speed gave Spitz his third gold medal and another world record: 1:52.78. By now, the local media had a nickname for him—der Hai, German for "the Shark."

On August 31, Spitz swam in the 100-meter butterfly. He won the race with another world-record time, 54.27. Later that day, he

Mark Spitz swam to a remarkable seven gold medals at the 1972 Games.

swam in another relay, the 4 x 200-meter freestyle. Once again, he was the team's last swimmer, and Spitz anchored another gold-medal-winning performance. The time of 7:35.78 was also another world record.

Good Enough for Seven?

By now, Spitz had won more gold medals at a single Olympics than any other U.S. swimmer, and he still had two events to go. He considered dropping out of the 100-meter freestyle. "It's

The butterfly was just one of the strokes Spitz mastered on his way to Olympic gold.

THE PRESSURE TO WIN

In 2000, Mark Spitz looked back at the 1972 Games and discussed his feelings as he entered the 100-meter freestyle.

It was the last of the four individual events, it was the sixth gold medal and on paper it was the event where I had the least amount of margin to win by. . . . The anguish and the torment I had to go through was overwhelming. Obviously I was having a great week, I had trained correctly and rested properly but the whole week of actually competing was starting to wear on me physically and emotionally. . . .

The 100-meter freestyle was known as the glamour event. If I hadn't won I would not have been known as the fastest swimmer in the world. There were 15 different swimming events and if I had won 14, whoever else won that event would have been recognized as the fastest swimmer.

tremendous," he said, "the pressure of not losing." He preferred to win every race he entered, and Spitz knew he faced a challenge from teammate Jerry Heidenreich in the 100. His coach told him, "If you don't swim the hundred meters, you might as well go home now. They'll say you're chicken." Spitz stayed in the race and won in 51.22, setting his sixth world record of the Games.

The next day was Spitz's last event, the 4 x 100-meter medley relay. In the medley, each swimmer on a team uses a different stroke. Swimming the butterfly, Spitz won his seventh medal, and the team set another world record, 3:26.42.

Spitz's feat in 1972 was historic: seven events, seven gold medals, seven world records. Unfortunately, the good feelings created by his triumphs were short. The day after Spitz won his last medal, Palestinian terrorists killed two Israeli athletes and kidnapped nine others. The incident marred what had been an exciting Olympics. Still, Spitz returned home a hero. No athlete has ever topped his mark of seven gold medals and seven world records at one Olympics.

Right: *A victorious Spitz with his gold medals.*

A DANGEROUS TIME

The murder and kidnapping of Israeli athletes in Munich worried Mark Spitz. The Palestinians had deliberately targeted Jewish athletes, and Spitz was Jewish. After his success, he was also famous, and perhaps a target for another terrorist attack. Arriving at a press conference, Spitz decided not to stand in front of the audience. "I'd be a perfect target for someone with a gun," he said. Instead, he sat down, surrounded by several U.S. coaches. Spitz left Munich before the end of the Games, as he and Olympic officials feared for his safety.

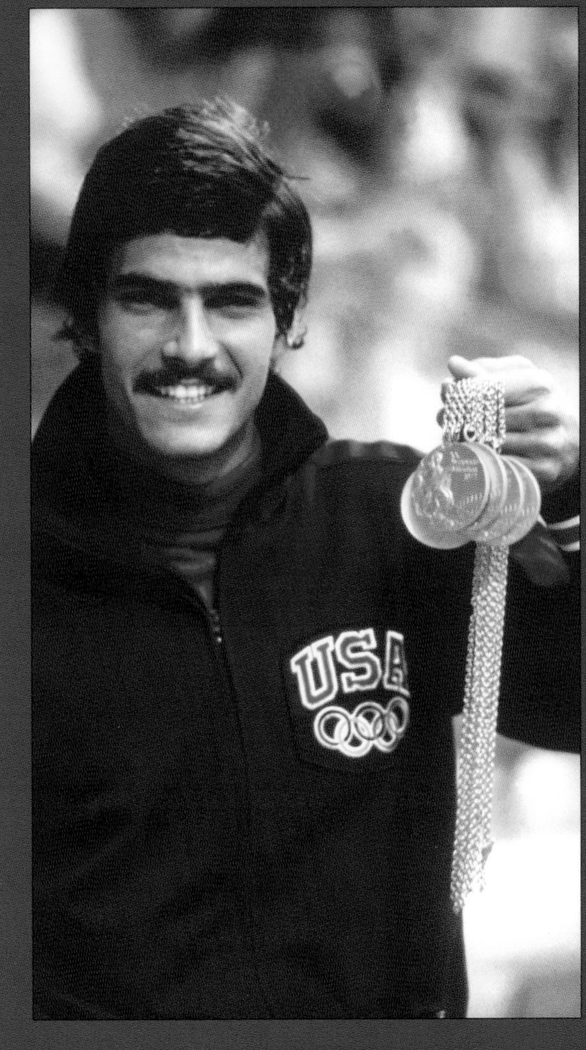

A PERFECT TEN

Nadia Comaneci Receives Seven Perfect Scores and Wins Three Gold Medals in Gymnastics at the 1976 Summer Olympics

Bela Karolyi, the future Romanian (and U.S.) national gymnastics coach, was looking for new gymnasts in the Romanian countryside when he stopped by an elementary school. He noticed two girls pretending to be gymnasts as they played. He saw something special in their movements, and he later said, "I knew I would never leave the school until I found those two little girls." One of the girls was six-year-old Nadia Comaneci.

Romania's Nadia Comaneci scored a first-ever 10 for her balance beam routine at the 1976 Olympics.

Within a year, Comaneci was attending Romania's new Gymnastic High School, spending half her day in classes and half in the gym. At the age of eight, she competed in the Romanian national championships. Although her performance on the beam was flawed, Comaneci helped her team win the championship. The next year, she won her first international event, and by 1975, at age thirteen, Comaneci was the European champion. Entering the 1976 Summer Games in Montreal, Canada, the 4-foot-11-inch (149-cm) gymnast thought she could do well. "I hoped for a medal," she said years afterward, "and possibly a gold one." No one, however, expected the perfection she demonstrated on her way to five Olympic medals.

A New Level

At the 1972 Games in Munich, Olga Korbut had won the adoration of fans. Korbut, a small, smiling Soviet gymnast, bubbled with emotion during and after her routines and captured three gold medals. She was also at the Montreal Games, and some members of the media tried to create a rivalry between Korbut and Comaneci. The Romanian, however, soon proved to be in her own class.

Comaneci's first event was the balance beam, as part of the team competition. She received a score of 9.9, then continued with good scores for the floor exercise and vault. Her last event on the first night of the team competition was the uneven bars. Comaneci flew from one bar to the other and back, keeping her tiny body perfectly controlled. Taking a last leap, she landed solidly. "I was not one for looking straight at the scoreboard," she later recalled, ". . . but I remember this incredible noise."

The noise was the buzz from the crowd as they realized the judges had given her a 10. To the judges, Comaneci had made every move flawlessly. Never before had an Olympic gymnast received that perfect score. On the second day of the team competition, Comaneci dazzled the judges again, this time on the beam. "Nothing,"

The Soviet Union's spritely and spirited Olga Korbut was a crowd favorite at the 1972 Olympics in Munich.

A PERFECT MOMENT

In her autobiography, Nadia Comaneci describes receiving her first perfect score.

The whole thing flowed like a dream. I was unaware of time or effort. Almost instinctively, my body slipped into its well rehearsed sequence of movements culminating in a good dismount. I knew it had been a good performance even before the reaction of the spectators invaded my concentration. . .

Suddenly an almighty roar went up and . . . I turned to look at the scoreboard—it showed that I had been awarded only one point! It registered 1.00, which in those days was the computer's way of announcing a perfect score. It was the first one in Olympic history. Pandemonium broke out around me, even other competitors rushed to congratulate me. I waved frantically at the cheering crowd.

she later wrote, "was going to stop me from demonstrating what I thought a beam exercise was all about. Nothing did." Once again, her precise flips and handstands earned a perfect score.

Bringing Home the Medals

Comaneci went again on the uneven bars, this time doing moves of her own choosing. Once again, she nailed a 10. Even with Comaneci's perfection, however, the Romanian team finished second in the event. If she were going to win a gold medal, Comaneci would have to do it in the individual competition.

The individual all-around title combines all the gymnastics events: beam, bars, floor exercise, and vault. On the beam and uneven bars, Comaneci again scored 10s. Also competing well was Nelli Kim of the Soviet Union, and she scored a 10 on the vault. Still, Comaneci's lead was too big, and she won the gold for the individual all-around.

Last up for the women gymnasts was the individual competition for each event. Comaneci had already shown her command of the uneven bars, and she did it one more time, earning another 10 and the gold medal. She then duplicated that performance on the beam, winning a 10 and the gold. She added a bronze in the floor exercise, just missing another 10.

The seven 10s and the five medals made

Comaneci brought a fun and innovative style to the floor exercise.

Comaneci the darling of the Games. Four years later in Moscow, she received less attention in North America because of the U.S. boycott. But Comaneci was still in top form, winning two more gold medals. Years after her Olympic success, Comaneci reflected back on her perfect scores in 1976: "I knew I had it in me to do a perfect routine but preparing for it in training and getting it absolutely right in front of 15,000 people are two quite different things."

ANOTHER SPECIAL 10

After retiring from competition, Nadia Comaneci eventually settled in the United States and married Bart Conner, a gold-medal winner for the U.S. gymnastics team in 1984. She and Conner began teaching gymnastics and then became involved with the Special Olympics, a competition for athletes with physical and mental disabilities. At the 1999 World Games in North Carolina, Comaneci awarded the gold medal in the balance beam to Cuba's Layanette Gonzalez—the first Special Olympics gymnast to score a perfect 10.

Comaneci showing off her gold.

MIRACLE ON ICE

The U.S. Ice Hockey Team Beats the Soviet Union on Its Way to Winning the Gold Medal at the 1980 Winter Olympics

In 1960, playing in front of a home crowd in Squaw Valley, California, the U.S. Olympic ice hockey team won the gold medal. The victory was surprising, but not totally shocking. The Americans had won a silver or bronze medal in every Olympics but two since the first Olympic hockey competition in 1920. (That year, the event was played at the Summer Games before switching to the Winter Games.) Still, the Soviet Union had taken the gold in 1956 and had been undefeated in international competition since then, so they were favored to win at Squaw Valley.

The U.S. hockey team in action against the Soviets at the 1980 Games.

After the 1960 Games, the Soviets reestablished themselves as the best national hockey team in the world. Featuring players from the Soviet army, the team won the next four Olympic gold medals. In 1979, the Soviets beat a team of National Hockey League (NHL) All-Stars, and they were the clear favorites to win another gold at the 1980 Games in Lake Placid, New York. Standing in their way were some determined U.S. college hockey players and their coach, Herb Brooks.

Building a Winner

Brooks, the coach at the University of Minnesota, had traveled to Russia and studied the Soviet style of play: long, accurate passes and fluid open-ice skating. His plan was to turn this style against the Russians, instead of using the typical North American tactics of dumping the puck into the opponent's zone and playing rough along the boards. He also knew the Americans had to match the conditioning of the Soviet athletes, who were famous for their stamina.

With this game plan, Brooks began assembling his players in 1979. Some were good enough to play in the National Hockey League. A few were college All-Americans. None, however, could match the best Soviet players in experience. To make up for that, Brooks trained them hard and demanded that they play better than they ever had before. "I admire your talents," he told them. "And I'll push you because I admire your talents."

To prepare for the Olympics, the U.S. team played NHL teams, college teams, and European teams. With one game to go, they had a record of 42–15–3. Their last opponents before the Olympics were the Russians. Playing at New York's Madison Square Garden, the Soviet squad crushed the Americans, 10–3. Soviet coach Viktor Tikhonov said, "I think the United States team has a very good future." No one, however, expected that future to start at Lake Placid. Brooks said he would be happy with a bronze medal.

The United States attempts to sneak the puck around the back of the goal as the alert Soviet goalie keeps tabs on the action.

Golden Moments

The U.S. team started the Olympics well, tying Sweden, then winning four games in a row. The Americans' hard training had paid off, as they outscored their opponents 24–10. A 7–3 victory against Czechoslovakia was especially impressive, as the Czechs had excelled in international hockey since 1972, twice winning the world championships.

With a record of 4–0–1, the Americans entered the medal round. Their first opponent: the Soviet team. The Russians scored first, but with six minutes to play in the first period, U.S. left winger Buzz Schneider tied the score. The Soviet team quickly regained the lead but could not hold it. With just one second on the clock, center Mark Johnson, the Americans' leading scorer, made it 2–2. For the second period, the Soviets replaced

Celebrating their victory over the Soviets, U.S. players pile on top of goalie Jim Craig, while John O'Callahan and Mike Ramsey collapse on the ice and Neal Broten jumps for joy.

star goalie Vladislav Tretiak with Vladimir Myshkin. The young replacement was effective, shutting out the Americans while his teammates added another goal. The Soviets peppered goalie Jim Craig with thirty shots in the first two periods, and his fine play kept the Americans in the game.

Before the last period, Brooks told his team, "Just stay with your system. Play your game." The Americans listened and kept skating hard. Almost nine minutes into the period, Dave Silk fed Johnson. The pass went off a Soviet skate onto Johnson's stick, and he blasted in his second goal of the game. Now the Americans knew they had a

FROM THE OLYMPICS TO THE PROS

Members of the 1980 U.S. Olympic team who went on to play in the NHL

Forwards and Defensemen	Seasons	GP	G	A	PTS	PIM
Bill Baker, D	3	143	7	25	32	175
Neal Broten, F	17	1033	289	634	923	569
Dave Christian, F	15	1009	340	433	773	284
Steve Christoff, F	5	248	77	64	141	108
Mark Johnson, F	11	669	203	305	508	260
Rob McClanahan, F	5	224	38	63	101	126
Ken Morrow, D	10	550	17	88	105	309
Jack O'Callahan, D	7	389	27	104	131	541
Mark Pavelich, F	7	355	137	192	329	340
Mike Ramsey, D	18	1070	79	266	345	1012
Dave Silk, F	7	249	54	59	113	271

Goaltenders	Seasons	GP	W	L	T	MINS	GA	SO	AVG
Jim Craig	3	30	11	10	7	1588	100	0	3.78
Steve Janaszak	2	3	0	1	1	160	15	0	5.63

chance to win. Barely a minute later, left winger Mike Eruzione took a shot from 25 feet (7.6 m) out. Myshkin, blocked by one of his own players, could not see the puck as it entered the net, giving the United States the lead. For the next ten minutes, the Americans played their usual tough defense. When the final buzzer sounded, the score was still 4–3. The Americans had done the impossible and beaten the Soviets. Known as the Miracle on Ice, the win has been called the greatest moment in U.S. sports history.

In the arena, the players celebrated on the rink while the fans cheered in the stands. Around the country, people who had been watching the game on TV also laughed and cried with joy. To some people, the game was about more than the chance to win a medal. The Cold War rivalry of the United States and the Soviet Union had carried over into athletics. The country with the better team might also be able to say it had the better system: the freedom and democracy of the United States versus the communism of the Soviet Union.

The U.S. team, however, did not have too much time to celebrate. It still had to play Finland, and there was still a chance the Americans might not win a medal. The Finns led 2–1 after two periods, but the Americans came back with three in the last period to win the game and the gold medal. The miracle was complete.

Following their stunning upset of the Soviets, the United States faced off against Finland for the gold. Here, the Americans acknowledge the crowd during the gold medal ceremony.

REMEMBERING THE MIRACLE

Years after the 1980 Olympics, people still go up to the U.S. gold-medal winners to thank them for the victory against the Soviet Union. Said Jim Craig in 1998, "Everywhere I go, people tell me where they were, what they were doing and how proud they were." Mike Eruzione told *Sports Illustrated* in 2000, "The first time you meet someone, they've got to tell you where they were. They'll say, 'Let me tell you a funny story. You'll never guess where I was when you guys [won].'. . . I've heard them all and they're great."

FIVE TIMES FAST

Eric Heiden Wins Five Individual Gold Medals at the 1980 Winter Olympics

In parts of Europe, speed skaters are superstars, as popular as the best quarterbacks and baseball sluggers are in the United States. American skater Eric Heiden was already famous among European speed-skating fans before the 1980 Winter Games in Lake Placid, New York. He had won the world championship in 1977, then successfully defended his title the next two years. In his homeland, however, Heiden was still virtually unknown. Five races at Lake Placid changed all that.

Eric Heiden preparing to race at the 1980 Olympics, where he would bring home five gold medals.

By the time the Games started, the media had learned of Heiden and his skills. Both he and his sister Beth, also a speed skater, had competed for the U.S. team at the 1976 Games in Innsbruck, Austria, but they had finished far behind the winners. This time, they were expected to win several medals, if not all golds. In the end, Beth brought home a bronze medal in the 3,000 meters.

Eric, as the world champion, received more attention than

Beth. He was going to attempt something done only once before in the Olympics—skate in all five speed-skating events. The races ranged from 500 meters to 10,000 meters and required different skills. Heiden had competed in these different races at the world championships, but at the Olympics, he would face racers skating only in their strongest events. "It'll be hard," he told reporters before the Games began. "The hardest races for me will be the 500, 5,000, and the 10,000."

Fast Start

Heiden's weakest event was the 500, and it was his first race of the Games. Racers skate on a large, oval rink two at a time, though they race against the clock, not each other. Skating next to Heiden was the world-record holder at 500 meters, Yevgeny Kulikov of the Soviet Union. The American barely noticed. He said, "I'm only concerned with what I do on the ice."

The starting gun fired, and the two skaters sped down the track. Kulikov took a short lead, then Heiden matched him. Going into the last turn, the Soviet skater was ahead again, but Heiden shot out of the turn and took the lead for good. His time of 38.03 seconds was a new Olympic record—and fast enough for the gold medal.

Heiden's next race was the 5,000 meters. Once again, he set a new Olympic record, skating in 7:02.29. Then he had to wait for the other skaters to go, to see if the time stood up. It did, and Heiden had his second gold. The third came in the 1,000 meters, his strongest event. He had set a world record of 1:14.99 in 1978, and topped that mark twice before the 1980 Games. At Lake Placid, Heiden won in 1:15.18, good enough for another Olympic record.

By now, the American fans cheered and shouted, "Eric, Eric!" every time Heiden stepped

Beth Heiden, a famed speed skater in her own right, with her brother Eric in February 1979.

TWO-SPORT CHAMPION

Eric Heiden's retirement from speed skating didn't end his interest in competitive sports. Both Heiden and his sister Beth turned to cycling. She won the 1980 world road race championship, while he won the professional U.S. cycling championship in 1985. Heiden also took part in the 2002 Winter Olympics in Salt Lake City, Utah, but this time he was on the sidelines. Now a surgeon, Heiden served as team doctor for the U.S. speed-skating team.

onto the ice. His opponents also respected his talents. Said one Soviet skater, "Eric Heiden is the greatest skater of the last twenty years." His next chance for gold came in the 1,500 meters. Skating next to Kai Arne Stenshjemmet of Norway, Heiden inched ahead. Then, rounding a turn, he slipped a bit, bringing a gasp from the crowd. Keeping his balance and the lead, Heiden finished the course in 1:55.44, once again winning in Olympic-record time.

The Longest Race

Last up for Heiden was the marathon of speed skating, the 10,000-meter event. During the long race, skaters cruise with both arms tucked behind their backs, swinging the outside arm only on turns. The skaters look relaxed, as if enjoying an afternoon skate on a backyard pond. The race, however, is grueling, as the skaters are bent over, their legs pumping, for more than 6 miles.

As Heiden waited for the starting gun, he knew what time he had to beat. Norwegian Tom Erik Oxholm had finished with 14:36.60—seven seconds faster than Heiden's best time ever at 10,000 meters. Heiden had overslept the night before, after watching the U.S. hockey team beat the Soviet Union in the game known as the Miracle on Ice. Now he needed a miracle of his own.

Heiden's superior leg strength served him well as both a speed skater and later a world-class cyclist.

Circling the track, Heiden fell behind Soviet skater Victor Leskin, the world-record holder. Slowly, however, Leskin lost speed, and Heiden seemed to finish each lap faster than the last. He crossed the finish line in 14:28.13, winning the gold and setting a new world record.

With his five victories, Heiden set a new record for the most individual gold medals at a single Olympics—Winter or Summer. Bothered by all the attention he received as a sports hero, Heiden retired from skating after the 1980 Games. The greatest speed skater of his era said, "I really liked it best when I was a nobody."

A HAPPY—AND PAINFUL—END

This Associated Press report describes Eric Heiden's last Olympic race.

The speed skating oval . . . was jammed with spectators hoping to see Heiden win his unprecedented fifth gold medal. They climbed trees, stood on top of buildings and portable toilets, climbed fences and peered from the top of cars as the gold-clad Viking sped the 10,000 meters, more than six miles. . . .

After he had raced 5,200 meters, Heiden took off like a shot. He pulled ahead and the crowd roared, waving flags and signs.

He finished the race and the record flashed on the scoreboard. Heiden went around another lap, still crouched over, obviously in pain. "I kept thinking how nice it was going to be to stand up again," he said.

Heiden, winner of the 1,500-meter event, with silver medalist Kai Arne Stenshjemmet (left) and bronze medalist Terje Anderson (right), both from Norway.

KING CARL'S GOLDEN TOUCH

Carl Lewis Wins Four Gold Medals at the 1984 Summer Games

When Carl Lewis was ten years old, he met Jesse Owens. Lewis was already running track, and as he progressed, he chose Owens as his role model. Perhaps the greatest track-and-field athlete of all time, Owens had won four gold medals at the 1936 Berlin Games. After that, no track athlete ever won four events at the same Olympics—until Lewis duplicated the feat at the 1984 Games in Los Angeles.

Lewis entered the Games with the intent of matching Owens, believing he could win gold medals in the 100- and 200-meter races, the long jump, and the 4 x 100-meter relay. Lewis was not boasting; he had already staked his claim as one of the greatest track stars since Owens. At age nineteen, he made the U.S. Olympic team, though he did not compete because of the U.S. boycott of the 1980 Moscow Games. The next year, Lewis was best in the world at both 100 and 200

Carl Lewis won four medals at the 1984 Olympics, including one here in the 200-meter race, matching the achievement of his childhood role model, Jesse Owens.

Lewis heading for a long jump at the 1984 Olympic Games.

meters, and he started a string of sixty-five consecutive wins in the long jump, a streak that eventually lasted ten years. Still, despite his obvious talents, Lewis was not always popular. Fellow track star Edwin Moses once said, "He rubs it in too much. A little humility is . . . what Carl lacks."

Cheers . . . and Boos

For his first event in Los Angeles, Lewis ran in the 100-meter event. He sprinted well in the qualifying heats and felt strong going into the finals. Teammate Sam Graddy took an early lead, but with 20 meters to go, Lewis blew by him and won by 8 feet (2.44 m)—a huge distance for such a short race. He finished with a time of 9.99 seconds. As Lewis took a victory lap, the crowd cheered and waved U.S. flags. At one point, Lewis took one of the flags and ran with it around the track. He later wrote, "This would be the most enjoyable victory lap of my life."

At the 1988 Games in Seoul, Carl Lewis won another gold medal in the long jump.

Two days later, Lewis came out for the long jump. Going into the wind, he went 28 feet $\frac{1}{4}$ inch (8.55 m) on his first jump. The second time around, he fouled. Since he had a commanding lead and two more races to run, Lewis decided to save energy and pass on his last four jumps. The crowd booed, wanting to see him go for the world record of 29 feet $2\frac{1}{2}$ inches (8.9 m) set by Bob Beamon in 1968. "I was shocked at first," Lewis said. "But after I thought about it I realized they were booing because they wanted see to more of [me]."

Lewis had hurt a leg muscle before the Olympics, another reason he decided not to take all his jumps. The injury still bothered him as he prepared for the finals of the 200-meter race. Still, Lewis ran well, and his time of 19.80 was one of his best ever—and a new Olympic record.

One Gold to Go

Lewis's last event was the relay, just as it had been for Owens forty-eight years before. Unlike Owens, who ran first, Lewis was the anchor, the last man to take the baton. The four American sprinters were favored to win, and they did with ease. When Lewis crossed the finish line in 37.83 seconds, he was 23 feet (7 m) ahead of the second-place finisher. The time was a new world record—the only one set at the 1984 Summer Games. Lewis had his fourth medal. "King Carl" had matched the great Jesse Owens.

Unlike Owens, Lewis competed again in the Olympics. In 1988, at Seoul, South Korea, Lewis defended his Olympic titles in the 100 meters and the long jump. The 100-meter gold came after some controversy. Even though Lewis ran his best time ever, he lost to Canadian Ben Johnson. Later, however, officials learned Johnson had taken an illegal drug, so they took away his gold medal and gave it to Lewis.

Lewis was on the U.S. Olympic team again in 1992, in Barcelona, Spain. He won his third straight gold in the long jump, then anchored the 4 x 100-meter relay team, which also won the gold. Four years later, at the age of thirty-five, Lewis tried out again for the U.S. team. He had lost a step or two as a sprinter, but he could still leap, and he was the third qualifier for the long-jump team.

At the 1996 Games in Atlanta, Georgia, Lewis put himself in the record books. His jump of 27 feet 10¾ inches (8.5 m) was good enough for the gold. This ninth victory tied the record for most gold medals in an Olympic career. It also made Lewis just the second athlete to win the same event in four consecutive Olympics, a mark he shares with U.S. discus thrower Al Oerter. Lewis ended his career not just as the greatest track star since Jesse Owens, but as one of the greatest athletes of all time.

THE ROAD TO THE ROSE BOWL

In his autobiography, *Inside Track*, Carl Lewis describes how he felt after the 1984 Summer Olympics.

There was joy—incredible joy—but more than that, there was relief. It was over—finally. There would be no more expectations, no more predictions, just four events, four victories. Period. What a relief! . . .

I was asked about the comparison between Jesse Owens and me—as I had been asked so many times—and I said: "Jesse Owens is still the same man he was to me before. He is a legend. I'm just a person. I still feel like the same Carl Lewis I was six years ago, except I'm a little older and a lot more people come to my press conferences."

A GOLDEN RECORD

Carl Lewis's nine gold medals and his winning results

1984	**100-meter race**	**9.99 seconds**
	200-meter race	**19.80 seconds**
	long jump	**28 feet ¼ inch**
	4 x 100-meter relay	**37.83 seconds**
1988	**100-meter race**	**9.92 seconds**
	long jump	**28 feet 7½ inches**
1992	**long jump**	**28 feet 5½ inches**
	4 x 100-meter relay	**37.40 seconds**
1996	**long jump**	**27 feet 10¾ inches**

SKATING'S TEEN QUEEN

Sarah Hughes Wins an Amazing Come-from-Behind Gold Medal at the 2002 Winter Games

In the Winter Olympics, figure skaters are often the most visible and the most popular competitors. On the ice, the best skaters combine physical skill with artistic expression. Entering the 2002 Games at Salt Lake City, Utah, U.S. skater Michelle Kwan was the favorite to win the women's competition. Kwan, a four-time world champion, was known for her graceful presence on the ice. At the 1998 Olympics in Nagano, Japan, she was upset by teammate Tara Lipinski, the youngest woman ever to win the figure skating gold medal. This time, most skating experts predicted, Kwan would skate to the top spot.

Sarah Hughes brought energy and excitement to her short program at the 2002 Winter Olympics in Salt Lake City.

Joining Kwan on the 2002 U.S. team were Sasha Cohen and Sarah Hughes. Hughes, sixteen years old, had been impressive in 2001. She beat Kwan and top Russian skater Irina Slutskaya at an international competition in

Canada and finished third at the world championships. But at the U.S. Nationals in January 2002, Kwan and Cohen finished ahead of Hughes and seemed more likely to win medals in Salt Lake City. To improve her chances, Hughes changed her routine. She added more difficult moves and skated to new, more dramatic music. She also came to the Games determined to do well. "I can't predict how I'm going to do," she said, ". . . but I'm not coming to the Olympics to be last."

The Skate of a Lifetime

The 2002 women's Olympic competition began on February 19 with the short program. Each skater completed a number of required jumps and spins while skating to music. Judges scored the skaters on how well they performed the required moves and on their artistic expression, using a scale of 0 to 6 for each category. Hughes, skating fifth out of twenty-seven skaters, made a few mistakes and received some low scores for her technical skills. She finished the short program in fourth place, behind Kwan, Slutskaya, and Cohen.

Two days later, the skaters prepared for the long program, or free skate. Each skater had four minutes to show the best of her talents. Hughes decided she would skate for fun, not worrying about how well she did. She said later, "I thought there was no way in the world I could win."

Among the leaders, Hughes went first. She smiled broadly as she spun and leapt across the ice, and the crowd's cheers grew louder with every successful move. Hughes did a triple-triple—two triple jumps in a row and one of the hardest moves in women's figure skating. A clean landing brought another roar from the audience. Then Hughes did a second triple-triple combination, and once again she

Hughes surprised the world with her virtually flawless performance in the free skate and stole the gold medal from the other contenders.

Sarah Hughes (center) with silver medalist Irina Slutskaya of Russia (right) and U.S. teammate Michelle Kwan (left), who won bronze.

was flawless. After finishing her skate, Hughes beamed as the crowd cheered and threw flowers at her feet.

To some skating experts at the rink, Hughes's performance was perfect. She later called it "the skate of my life." The judges' scores, however, were not as high as they could have been—mostly 5.8s for both technical ability and artistic expression. Now Hughes would have to see if she had done well enough to win a medal.

Golden Moment

Hughes and her coach, Robin Wagner, waited in a locker room as the other skaters performed their routines. Cohen fell doing a triple-triple combination, ending her chances for a medal. Hughes was guaranteed at least a bronze. Kwan went next. She only needed a good performance, not a great one, to hold on to first place and win the gold medal. But like Cohen, Kwan fell during a jump. Still, even with that error, Kwan had a chance to stay in first, if Slutskaya finished behind both Hughes and Cohen.

Slutskaya was famous for her energetic style and strong athletic talent. That night in Salt Lake City, however, she was slow and did not land cleanly on several jumps. Despite a less-than-perfect performance, four judges awarded her first place for the long program, but her overall score put her in second place.

As Hughes and Wagner watched from the locker room with cameras pointed at them, at first they weren't sure what the results of those close scores were. But when they realized Hughes had won the gold, they let out screams of joy and disbelief. It was true—the gold medal was hers.

Enjoying her unlikely victory, Hughes told reporters, "I didn't hold back. I just skated for the fun of it." Hughes's performance and her bubbly personality made her the darling of the 2002 Winter Games. And with her gold medal, she could speak confidently about her future—"I think this is really just the beginning of my career."

JUDGES ON TRIAL

Before Sarah Hughes's victory, the skating events at the 2002 Olympics received more attention for the judges' scores than the skaters' jumps and spins. In the pairs event, Canadian skaters Jamie Salé and David Pelletier (left) thrilled the crowd and seemed to outperform Russians Yelena Berezhnaya and Anton Sikharulidze (right), but the Russians won the gold medal. After the event, French judge Marie Reine Le Gougne said she had been pressured to favor the Russians, presumably in exchange for favorable votes in other events—which, of course, is against Olympic rules. The judge was suspended and, amid debate and controversy, world skating officials decided to award a second gold medal in the event to Salé and Pelletier.

The controversy highlighted the difficulty of judging an event such as figure skating. The judges have guidelines they follow, but in the end, their opinions shape the score they give. In the past, judges have been accused of giving in to political or social pressure to vote a certain way. Skating officials now hope to improve judging standards to avoid this problem at future Games.

The questions about judging also touched the women's event. After Irina Slutskaya won the silver medal, Russian officials said bad judging cost her the gold. The Russians filed a protest, but it was not allowed.

Olympics Time Line

776 B.C. The first recorded Olympic Games are held in Greece.

1896 The first modern Olympics are held in Athens, Greece.

1912 Women are allowed to compete in the Olympics for the first time, at the Summer Games in Stockholm, Sweden.

1924 The first Winter Games are held in Chamonix, France; distance runner Paavo Nurmi of Finland wins five gold medals at the Summer Games in Paris, France.

1936 Jesse Owens wins four gold medals in track and field at the Berlin Games; basketball is played at the Olympics for the first time, and the United States wins the gold medal.

1968 Bob Beamon sets a world record at the 1968 Games in Mexico City; U.S. medal winners Tommie Smith and John Carlos protest unequal treatment of African Americans.

1972 Swimmer Mark Spitz wins seven gold medals at the Games in Munich, Germany; the U.S. basketball team loses the gold medal—and its first Olympic game ever—in a controversial game with the Soviet Union; eleven Israelis die during and after a terrorist attack by Palestinians.

1976 At the Montreal Summer Games, Nadia Comaneci receives the first perfect score ever awarded to an Olympic gymnast.

1980 Eric Heiden wins five gold medals in speed skating at the Lake Placid Olympics; the U.S. hockey team upsets the heavily favored Soviet team on its way to winning the gold medal; the United States boycotts the Summer Games held in Moscow.

1984 The Soviet Union boycotts the Summer Games held in Los Angeles; Carl Lewis wins four gold medals, duplicating the success of Jesse Owens at the 1936 Games.

2000 Aboriginal sprinter Cathy Freeman wins a gold medal at the Sydney Games, bringing attention to race relations in Australia.

2002 U.S. figure skater Sarah Hughes comes from behind to charm the world and win the gold medal at the Winter Games in Salt Lake City, Utah; a judging controversy results in double gold medals being awarded in the pairs skating competition.

To Learn More

BOOKS

Anderson, Dave. *The Story of the Olympics.* Revised edition. New York: William Morrow, 2000.

Herran, Thomas and Joe. *The Grolier Student Encyclopedia of the Olympic Games.* Danbury, Conn.: Grolier Educational, 1996.

Italia, Bob. *100 Unforgettable Moments in the Winter Olympics.* Edina, Minn.: Abdo & Daughters, 1996.

Oxlade, Chris, and David Ballheimer. *Olympics*. New York: Dorling Kindersley, 2000.

Streissguth, Tom. *Jesse Owens.* Minneapolis: Lerner, 1999.

The U.S. Olympic Committee. *Olympism: A Basic Guide to the History, Ideals and Sports of the Olympic Movement.* Glendale, Calif.: Griffin Publishing, 1996; Milwaukee: Gareth Stevens Publishing, 2001.

INTERNET SITES

Great Olympians
www.greatolympians.com
Focuses on track-and-field athletes and includes current information on track-and-field sports.

The International Olympic Committee
www.olympic.org
The official site of the governing body of the Summer and Winter Olympics has a museum and information on upcoming Games.

Olympic Results
www.ex.ac.uk/cimt/data/olympics/olymindx.htm
Sponsored by a British educational center, includes results from every Summer Olympics, plus a list of current Olympic records in track-and-field events.

Study Web – Olympic Sports
www.studyweb.com/Sports_Entertainment/Olympic_toc.htm
Designed especially for students and provides links to information on every Olympic sport.

The United States Olympic Committee
www.usolympicteam.com
To find information on past and present U.S. Olympians and read tips from such stars as soccer player Kristine Lilly and snowboarder Tom Czechin.

The U.S. Olympic Hall of Fame
www.usoc.org/halloffame/whatis.html
For information on athletes in the Hall of Fame.

Index

ABOUT THE AUTHOR

As an editor at Weekly Reader *for six years, Michael Burgan created educational material for an interactive online service and wrote on current events. Now a freelance author, Michael has written more than thirty books, primarily for children and young adults. These include biographies of Secretary of State Madeleine Albright, Presidents John Adams and John F. Kennedy, and astronaut John Glenn. His other historical writings include two volumes in the series on American immigration and a series of four volumes on the Cold War. Michael has a bachelor of arts degree in history from the University of Connecticut and resides in that state.*